What a Nightmare:
Growing Up in Spanish Harlem

Gloria Saunders

PublishAmerica
Baltimore

© 2006 by Gloria Saunders
All rights reserved. No part of this book may be reproduced, stored in a retrieval system or transmitted in any form or by any means without the prior written permission of the publishers, except by a reviewer who may quote brief passages in a review to be printed in a newspaper, magazine or journal.

First printing

At the specific preference of the author, PublishAmerica allowed this work to remain exactly as the author intended, verbatim, without editorial input.

ISBN: 1-4241-2265-1
PUBLISHED BY PUBLISHAMERICA, LLLP
www.publishamerica.com
Baltimore

Printed in the United States of America

What a Nightmare:
Growing Up in Spanish Harlem

Gloria Saunders

I was born in Queens, New York. My parents were born in Puerto Rico. My mother, Angela, was born in Santurce, Puerto Rico. My mother spoke fluent English. My father Victor did not. He never did learn the language. I had two brothers. My younger brother is named Johnny. My older brother was named Victor, Jr. I also had one sister named Lillian. We were all two years apart.

When I was four years old, which is as far back as I can remember, we moved to 110th Street, between Lexington and Third, Ave., New York. I recall sitting on a window sill in the living room. I was looking down across the street to the grocery store my parents owned. I was feeling lonely and sad, because I was left alone often. I was left alone because my mother had no one to take care of me. When she could get away from the store, she would come up to check up on me and give me something to eat. We lived on the third floor of an apartment building. She finally hired an older lady to take care of me. My sister and two brothers were attending school.

My parents' grocery store did not do well. My mother was a very kind and sympathetic person. She gave credit to numerous people who never paid back. This made my father angry. He was always yelling at her because of this. My mother was always upset so she started drinking beer. That is the reason she started to go downhill. My father also drank, but not excessively. After they lost the business, she went to work at a factory. My father would wait outside of the factory so she could give him her paycheck. He finally got a job in a factory, polishing silverware. While they worked my sister Lillian took care of us. Lillian was only twelve years old. She would give us chores to do. My younger brother and I took turns doing the dishes. My older brother Victor was hanging out looking for drugs. He was fourteen. First he started smoking marijuana and then he went to heroin. He was introduced to drugs by this guy named Gorilla. Most of us had nicknames. Mine was Pretzel because I was so skinny. They also called me Pepsi because I drank a lot of Pepsi. Victor had been an altar boy in the Catholic Church. He was a very well behaved boy until he started taking drugs. He had asthma, which made him unhappy since he was always coughing.

We lived in Spanish Harlem. The people that lived on our block were mostly Puerto Ricans. The people that lived on 111th street were Italians. Sometimes, they would come into our block and start shooting their guns at us. We would all run in different directions. One day they shot two of my friends. Thank God, they were not killed. The reason they did this was that they considered us to be different. We called them guineas and they called us spics. At that time, Puerto Ricans were coming more and more to the United States. Some of them did not speak English. We also came from a different culture. A lot of nationalities did not like us. The Italians came to our block to start trouble just about every couple of days. When I saw them coming I ran into a building to hide. A Puerto Rican boy was with the rival gang that day. He followed me and told me to hide and not come out. I was surprised to see a Spanish boy in that gang. Months later he came to see me. I liked him. We went to his friend's house. He told me his friend was home, but when we got there, his friend wasn't there. He started to kiss me, then he pushed me on the bed and wanted to make love to me. I was very frightened. I did not dare yell. I scratched his face and pushed him off me. I ran out of the apartment. The next day my brother asked him who scratched his face and he said a cat did it. I said nothing. I knew if I told my brother there would be a lot of trouble. I did not want to cause any problems. We lived in a very bad neighborhood. Drinking, drugs, gang fights and lots of loud music. The loud music I did not mind. It made my spirit and soul come alive. My parents and my sister did not allow me to leave the block. In fact I was not allowed to go out to play because the area was so bad. My father would hit me on the legs with his belt so that I would not go out to play.

    We played in the street, as the cars drove by. We played "kick the can", "running bases", "ring—go—li—ri—oh coca—cola" and "Johnny on the pony". I used to hang out in the candy store. My father did not want me to go there. One night, the lady of the candy store asked me to go with her to buy some figs. She said she was going to make home-made whiskey. In Spanish it is called "mata rata" which means to kill rats. She sold this whiskey in the back of the store for 50 cents a shot. That night her husband gave me my first drink. I had a couple more after that. It was 8:00 when my father came looking for me. I was drunk but he did not notice. Walking home, I tried to stay far behind so that he would not smell the liquor on my breath. When I went to bed, the room started to spin. I threw up. I was up most of the night throwing up and then I had to wash the sheets so no one would know that I had been drinking. I was very quiet, so I wouldn't wake my father. I was only ten years old and swore I would never drink again.

During the years of my going to school I was always afraid that I was going to get jumped by a gang of kids. The school was on 106th street. Since I lived four blocks away I would walk by myself but was afraid the kids would bother me. I was a good student and got A's and B's.

The gang fights became more difficult when I started junior high school. The school was much closer, so I only had to walk one block. Leaving the school building at the end of the day was not easy. The black girls would be waiting to beat us up. I finally joined a gang so that I would have protection from the other gangs. I knew a girl named Toni, who gave me heroin to try and I used it three times. The last time I used it, I decided not to do it anymore. I knew it was bad for me. I also saw what it was doing to my brother Victor. I felt bad for him because the habit was getting worse.

I started smoking cigarettes when I was fourteen years old. I smoked in the school bathroom. The principal came into the bathroom and caught us. The other girls started to blow the smoke out the window.

I ran into the bathroom stall and got up on the seat so that my legs would not show and closed the door. I prayed she would not catch me. Then I heard her say, "who is there"? I said "It's me, Gloria". She sent me to her office and I stayed there the whole day. When she returned at the end of the day, I had fallen asleep. She woke me up and sent me back to class, she had forgotten why I was there. That was a close call!

In the seventh grade I had a substitute teacher. His name was Mr. Carr. He taught our class for three days. He was trying to teach but the girls were disruptive and noisy. He told me he would never teach a girl's school again. I told him not to worry that I would teach class for him. I had my two best friends with me. Tata, was her nickname for Carmen and Estelle. Meanwhile Amparo, a

WHAT A NIGHTMARE: GROWING UP IN SPANISH HARLEM

Puerto Rican girl was dancing rhumba, a Spanish dance. She was wiggling her butt, and she had a huge butt. The other girls played the drums to the rhythm of her beat. We used our desk as drums. Poor Mr. Carr, I thought he was going to cry. The classroom was a riot. The bell rang and we changed classes. As I was going down the stairs this big black girl told me I had better get out of her way. I asked her what was she going to do about it. I didn't, and kept walking. I was really scared but didn't want her to know. She was big and tough and I was short and skinny. I made friends with this black girl named Clara. She could fight better than any of the other girls. I saw her beat two girls at one time. I realized at that time that when a black girl is by herself she is not so tough, but when they are with their friends, they are ready to fight at the drop of a hat, at that time we were all in the minority group. We still are but we have more opportunities now.

When I reached the age of 10, I noticed my mother and father were having problems. My mother was a very pretty woman and my father was very protective. When he came home, after a day of work, he would listen to the gossip of the neighbors that my mother had been out all day. She would sometimes go out with her girlfriend. By the time he reached the third floor he would be furious. He would walk in yelling and would slap her. As time went on it got worse. He was always slapping and punching her. One day he broke her collarbone. Another day he hit her with a frying pan. I would cover my ears to stop the yelling and get on my knees and cry. She began to have a great fear of him. Eventually, she left him. I really missed my mother something awful. I adored her. We all missed her. That is when my sister took over the role of a mother. She was twelve years old. She disciplined us. Took care of us. Cooked cleaned and ironed. She was the best. I guess my brother Johnny was imitating my father. He started slapping me around if I so much as spoke to a boy. He became very protective toward me. He showed me how to box so no one would hurt me. My brother Victor started mainlining heroin. He could not control his addiction. He was very young. In order to support his habit, he had to steal. He stole my father's suits. My father told him he had to go live with my mother. Eventually, Victor went to jail. He also went to different programs for his addictions. He could not kick the habit no matter how hard he tried. Lillian and I had him stay home with us. He tried cold turkey. Cold turkey is a form of kicking the habit without medication. He was sick for three days. He had cramps and cold sweats, but to no avail. He would always go back to the streets and start all over again. My mother moved to a 102nd street with her friend. My father would only give her $20.00 a week so that she could cook dinner for all four of us. Everyday, my father would give me 12 cents so that I could catch the bus to go and eat at my mother's house. I was usually playing in the street and did not want to stop. I would take the money and buy a potato sandwich for dinner. I would then disappear around the corner for about an hour so that my father would not know that I did not go to my mother's house. Other times I would go to Estelle's house. Her grandmother felt sorry for me and would give me food. She knew I was hungry. Most of the time I was hungry, because a sandwich was not enough.

My father talked bad about my mother to my sister Lillian. She would get so upset that she would threaten to throw herself in front of a car if he did not stop. He finally stopped.

My mother was now drinking very heavily. When my father got angry, he would send us to her house to stay. She would start drinking early in the morning. She kept her bottle hidden in the clothes hamper. Her disposition was so bad when she was high, yet she was sweet and loving when she was sober. I didn't like to see her drink. One night, my mother was drinking. She told me and Lillian to go to my father's house. We were angry and hurt that she had asked us to leave. Instead we went to my friend Tata's house. Tata was on her own and living alone. Tata and I went out dancing and left Lillian behind. When we came back, there was blood all over the place. Lillian told us she fell. We found out later that she had been raped by a friend of ours. I never did find out what the whole truth was.

On the Christmas of 1945, I got an iron and a ironing board. I was so happy because I did not have many toys. Lillian told me that she had been to the P.A.L. They had provided us with toys. The P.A.L. is an organization that helps the needy. We were poor. My father would tell me to go to Tom's house, when I needed a pair of shoes. Tom lived up the block from us. He was a very good person. Whenever I needed something Tom would buy it for me. He became my godfather. Not officially, but that is what I chose to call him. He was Italian. His real name was Cayatano Grimaldi. He lived with a friend. Tom never married or had children. He made homemade wine in his basement. My brothers and I would help him make it. We would put the grapes in a squeezer and pull a handle. He also cooked for his male friends every Sunday. This is how he made his living. My mother would send me to Tom's house for whiskey. Tom gave me whiskey to bring to my mother but on the way I dropped it. My friends were there and I was embarrassed. He treated me better than my own father, even though I did not like him giving my mother liquor. Every Thursday, we would take the train to New Jersey and have dinner at his sister's house. Tom passed away when I was fourteen years old. He hemorrhaged from the nose. That was my first experience with a loved one leaving me.

I had my first summer job when I was fifteen. I worked in a doll factory making $30.00 a week. I told the employer that I was eighteen. I do not know how he believed me. I guess he was desperate for help. I spent practically my whole paycheck at the candy store. I was always treating my friends who had no money.

In 1955 I was fifteen and attended Washington Irving High School. I had several boyfriends growing up, but not one could compare to my boyfriend Tony. He was one of the best dressed boys on the block and the cutest. Several times he rode the train with me to school. I was very impressed with Tony because he had stopped using drugs. I was so happy with him. Things were going good for us until he decided to go back to 110th street, where most of the drug dealers were. He got high but his body couldn't handle it. He had been clean for a while and he couldn't handle his usual dose. He overdosed and died that night. I called his house the next day. I was told of his death by his mother. I never was able to attend the funeral because he lived to far away.

As I got older, my brothers and sister went in different directions. Johnny went into the Navy. He said he wanted to be in a different environment. Victor got a job. He was still using drugs. He only dated one girl that I knew of. He was too involved in the drug scene to really care for one particular girl. He never married. His life was a horrible mess. I loved him so much, but there was nothing I could do for him. One night he awoke me to take him to the hospital. He had been shot on his thigh, near his groin. From a handsome young man, he had turned into a sad looking person. Lillian went to work in an office. She was doing well until she met a guy who had come from Puerto Rico. His name was Orlando but everyone called him

Bellon which means nickel in Spanish. I think they called him that because he was so cheap. They got married after Lillian got pregnant. He started to use drugs and Lillian started to drink because she was so unhappy. She loved him very much but he was a thief and he did not want to work. She finally left him when she was eight months pregnant. At that time, I was working in a printing company and she came to live with me. She started to drink even heavier. When the baby was born she left her with my mother.

   I met Bob in the printing company I was working for. He was the foreman. I was seventeen years old. I quit school in the eleventh grade, that was the reason I went to work as an operator of a printing machine. Bob was married and had a daughter. He was nine years older than me. He was German and his wife was Puerto Rican. He told me that there was no love between him and his wife. He said that they did not sleep together anymore. I had my doubts about that. We started dating. I was not happy going out with a married man. After we were finished with work, Bob would usually invite me out to the bar for a drink. We would have shots and beer chasers. If we weren't drinking at the bar, we would go to my mother's house. We knew we could always drink there. Lillian, Victor, my mother, and I would sit around talking and drinking. I started to get tired of drinking so often. I told Bob I was leaving him. I told him we never went to movies or out to eat. I told him all he wanted to do was get high. I realized he had a problem. At that time there was no such thing as A.A. or detox programs. At least, not that I knew of. People were always high on alcohol or drugs. That was the environment that I had to contend with, and it really made me angry. Since I was young, I thought his drinking would pass. He had been in the Navy. I assumed this was his way of life.

When I told him I did not want to go out with a married man, he started to cry. He told me he would get a divorce. He also said that it was going to be hard for him to give up his four year old daughter Angela. Bob and I did well at the printing company. Our employer Ira asked us to move to Chicago to open up a new factory. I trained the girls to operate the printing machines. Bob was in charge of the whole company. Bob and I started living together. My sister Lillian was upset that I had moved to Chicago. I felt that for once I was entitled to a better life. One day, the florist delivered flowers to my house. He told me he had another bouquet for Bob's wife in New York. When Bob came home I was very upset. He told me the flowers were for mother's day. Then and there I decided to leave Chicago. I had developed Rheumatoid arthritis. It was very cold in Chicago. It snowed the whole nine months I was there. I went back to the Bronx and Bob stayed in Chicago. I was not feeling good about myself because I had told my family that I had been living in a furnished room. They did not know that I had been living with Bob. When I met Bob I was a virgin. I was sad and I felt cheated that he had not married me. I went back to work for Mr. Kristel in the printing company.

Working in a factory was not easy. I had to print two hundred thousand envelopes or more a day. I stood on my feet all day. Walking back and forth putting envelopes into one end of the machine, and packing them on the other end. My hands were always dirty from the ink. My feet got dirty from the dust on the floor. At the end of the day, I had to walk a distance to catch the bus to go home.

I enrolled in Barbazon modeling school in New York. Attending modeling school was one of the most rewarding events of my life. I felt as though I was a celebrity when I would leave my house to go to the school. I would dress to kill, with a big black hat box, high heels and a beautiful dress. Boy, did I look like a model. I worked during the week and attended school on weekends. I could barely afford the fee for the school and the clothes, but I was determined to succeed and leave the factory. I was taught how to walk properly, talk more refined, apply my makeup, arrange my hair differently. The whole treatment. Finally graduation night had arrived. All my classmates and I were dressed in black. We stood as statues on the platform. I was so anxious and excited. I felt that I could barely breathe. I felt as though pins were going throughout my body as I stood posing for the audience. Lillian and Bob were there on my graduation night. When I received my diploma I felt proud and beautiful. The following week I went to look for a modeling position. One employee asked me if I was interested in Screen Modeling. I said yes! He then proceeded to tell me it was nude modeling. I definitely did not want that job. The next place I was told I needed to be at least five feet and six inches tall. I was only five feet and three inches tall. Needless to say, there went my dreams up in smoke. I was also told that there was quite a bit of competition in the modeling field. I was devastated. At this time the arthritis made my ankles swollen, therefore, I was unable to wear high heels.

My career as a model was shattered. I returned to the printing company. I was determined to learn as much as I could of the printing industry. Bob and I were together again. We got an apartment in the Bronx. Bob was a hard worker. He treated me good, but we were still not married. I decided to do something about it.

Bob went to see his daughter. It was 9:00 p.m. and he had not returned. I went to his wife Carmen's house. He was talking with her and they had a good conversation going. I knocked on the door. She asked me in and offered me a chair. I stayed for about two hours, but I never sat down. She told me never to hurt her daughter. She told me that there was nothing between her and Bob. I told her I would never hurt her daughter. I told her that Bob had to make up his mind, after four years, it was her or I. Bob chose me. We went home together. Bob applied for a divorce. We went to North Carolina, where he was from, and got married. At the time I was twenty years old. We lived on Bryant Avenue in the Bronx.

Since Bob's first wife was Puerto Rican, this did not go well with the family. They were from the South, North Carolina. There you were black or white. No in between. When they first met me, they were displeased that I was also Puerto Rican. Whenever we went to visit his sister in North Carolina, people always looked at me as if I were different. I do not think they knew what Spanish was. After visiting the South for the fifth time, I had had enough of the prejudice. I told Bob that I wished I could get into a tub of bleach water and turn white, so they would not stare at me. I have an olive complexion.

A man asked me where did I get such a beautiful tan. I told him I was born with it. My sister-in-law told me they stared because I was pretty with my long black hair and dark brown eyes. I said "bull"!

The last time Bob saw his father, he told him he would not visit his grave, when he passed away. That is how his father made him feel. His mother was a wonderful woman. His mother showed me how to cook the best Thanksgiving dinner ever. She died from cancer. His sisters were great to me.

When Bob and I first met, he told me he would become Puerto Rican for me. Well he did! He was a German from North Carolina who could now dance merengue and any other type of Spanish dance. He learned how to cook rice, beans, and roast pork, which is the specialty in our type of food. He tried his best to speak Spanish. He was quite a character.

We had parties every weekend. Our neighbors in the building always came. We had lots of good times.

Bob bought me a black poodle. We named her Buttons. She was like a child to us. I mated her with another poodle, and she had three puppies. I went into the breeding business for a awhile. I really enjoyed it.

On weekend's Bob's daughter would come to stay with us. Her and I became extremely close. I loved her and taught her as much as I could, while she was growing up. Bob continued to drink heavily. On one occasion he did not come home to sleep. I suspected that he was seeing someone else. I went to see if he was in the girl's house. If he was, he sneaked out when he heard that I was at the door. I am sure he cheated on me. He never did admit it.

By the time my mother was forty eight years old, she had become an alcoholic. At that time, there was no help for alcoholics. At least not that I knew of. I went to speak to a priest of the Catholic Church to see if he could help my mother. He told me if she continued to drink, she would die. I left the church very disappointed with his answer. I lost faith in the church, but not in God. I was now working in an office building as a typist. This was my first office position, and I loved it. I worked the switchboard during the operator's lunch hour. I was working the switchboard one day when I received a call that my mother was in the hospital. She had major surgery on her stomach. When I arrived, she was in a coma. My cousin Sylvia was there. I became upset when she said my mother should stop drinking. She made this remark by my mother's bedside. I was told that people can hear when they are in a coma. My mother passed away that week. At the wake we were all there except Lillian. My sister could not be found. I was now taking care of her baby. I received a call from Lillian two weeks after the funeral. She was devastated that she did not know about our mother's death. She came to pick up her baby, Diana. She looked awful from the drinking. She took Diana to her mother-in-law's house. For the next two years Lillian lived with a boyfriend. She was doing very bad. I was feeling heart broken at the way my family turned out. I went to church to pray every day, on my lunch hour. I prayed that my family life would get better. I missed Lillian something awful. She was the world to me. I could not find her after a while. Johnny came to see me to tell me that Lillian was at the morgue. We went to identify her. The day of her wake, I was told by a friend of hers that her boyfriend had given her rubbing alcohol to drink. That is what killed her. She was twenty eight at the time of her death. Her daughter was sent to Puerto Rico to live with her father.

Johnny returned home from the Navy after four years. I only got to see him on his leave of absence. He was doing very well. The Navy had made a man out of him. I was very proud of him. He married a girl named Emma. She had a son named Gregory. After a while Johnny started going out by himself. Finally, Emma got tired of it and started to date a policeman. Their marriage ended in divorce.

I was unable to have children. I was not ovulating. I really wanted to have a baby. I told Bob that we should adopt. He did not want to in the beginning. After awhile, he gave in. We did not have any luck adopting in the Bronx.

Ira asked us to go to California to operate a new factory. I told Bob that we would have more of a chance of adopting out there. We moved to California and applied for an adoption. We were put on a two year waiting list. We bought a house. It had three bedrooms, two fireplaces, kitchen, living room, and garage. Bob did not want to buy it at first. I told him it was better than paying rent. We decorated a bedroom waiting for the arrival of our baby.

California was a beautiful place. It had the tallest palm trees and it was sunny every day. It was breath taking. It only rained two weeks out of the year. We did well at the factory. After the factory was running smoothly I went to work for two lawyers. When I lived in the Bronx I had attended a business school. I developed good skills and was a pretty good secretary. I enjoyed doing office work. It was so different from working as a printer. Bob came to my office and put a key on my desk. He asked me to look out the window. There was a brand new Mustang out there. I was overjoyed. When I arrived in California, I realized I would have to take driving lessons. I was twenty-five years old and had never driven before. After fifteen lessons, I finally got the hang of it. Even though it was beautiful in California, I missed New York. It was not easy to make friends and I missed my old friends. People were friendly but only on the outside. They said hello, but that was the extent of it. We finally did make friends with two married couples. Emily and Les and Marge and Pete. They were the best friends anyone could have. We enjoyed each other's company. We bought a boat and went fishing quite often. We also went camping.

I was busy cooking one day when I received a call from Johnny. He told me that Victor had been murdered. Victor had stopped using drugs and had taken to drinking. On 111th street, in the basement, there was an argument between him and two other men. They threw him into a burning hot furnace. He was burnt from the waist up. The police were able to identify him from his wallet in his back pocket. The lower part of his body had not been burnt. The police never found the men who killed him. I took the plane to the Bronx to attend the funeral. The casket was closed. He was thirty three years old. It was good to see Johnny and my father again. I also saw relatives and friends. It took me years to recover from the deaths in my family. Johnny had remarried to his new wife, Diana. They live in New Jersey. We decided to have all my family buried in New Jersey.

I took the plane back to California. I was heartbroken about my brother Victor. Such a tragic and horrible death. But God works in mysterious ways. I was home for a few days when I got a call from the adoption agency. We had been approved. I felt that God had taken one life, yet given me another. This was such a big event in our lives. When we arrived the social worker had a beautiful baby girl for us. As I held her on my lap she peed. She looked like Bob. Blonde hair and blue eyes. I am brunette with brown eyes and an olive complexion. When I took her home I was anxious and excited. Everything she did I wrote down in her baby book. I was thrilled with her. We named her Kim Lee. She was one month old when we got her. Bob was a good father and husband, but he drank every night. I started to join him. I knew I had to take care of the baby, therefore, I did not over do it. I should not have been doing it at all, but he bought a bottle to have at dinner every night. He never missed a day of work. His employer was not happy with his performance. We lived in California for six years. I became a foster parent when Kim was three years old. I had two girls, Betty Jean and Sheila. Betty Jean saw her mother killed by her father. She called me mommy the first day she came to live with us.

California is known for its earthquakes. I had the experience of being in about six. It was not a good feeling. It was a very scary feeling. I knew people who had lived there most of their lives and were used to the earthquakes. I could never get used to it. The day we went to Tennessee, there was a huge earthquake. There was a crack in the ceiling of our house. The chandelier shook. Kim's crib moved inches away from the wall. We went to Tennessee that same day to see the new factory that Bob was going to work in. There were thirteen tremors after that. We stayed in Tennessee for a week. We returned to California. We sold our house. We moved all the furniture to Tennessee and lived there for two years. The people were friendlier than California. Tennessee is a beautiful state. Green pastures and beautiful hills. I was not working at this time. I stayed home with Kim. The arthritis had affected my feet. My toes were crooked. I had surgery performed to straighten out my toes, on both feet. I had a lady name Barnette come and help me with Kim and to do the housework. She had raised thirteen children, but did not know how to do housework. She was such a good person, I decided to keep her. I taught her how to cook and take care of the house.

On our way home from church, Bob wanted to go to the bootlegger to buy whiskey. The liquor store was closed on Sunday. We happened to meet a farmer taking his horse to pasture. The horse was pregnant. I asked him if she was for sale? He said I could buy her for fifteen dollars. I gave him fifteen dollars. He charged me one dollar to deliver her to my house. I knew some men who had a farm, a few blocks from my house. They said we could leave her there for a case of beer per week. I named the horse Princess. When she had the colt, I named her Glory, after me.

Bob worked at the new branch, but was still drinking. He was getting worse. I tried to get him help, but he was too far gone. He was having hallucinations and the shakes. During the week he was not too bad because he was busy working. On weekends he drank constantly and slept all the time. He did not eat much. He only wanted to eat bread and milk. On weekends, I always had the blinds down so the neighbors would not come to visit us, since he was always sleeping. I did not want anyone to know he was drunk. It became such a horrible problem. People notice he had a drinking problem. I could not admit to myself that the man who meant everything to me was an alcoholic. I was also drinking along with him, but I knew I had to take care of my little girl. Therefore, I kept it pretty much under control because of her. I also knew I should stop, but it was becoming an addiction to me. I spoke to my best friend Aida in New Jersey. We were very close, like sisters. She told me that Bob was an alcoholic. She told me to go to A.A. and get him help. I was so hurt and confused, when she said this. I was in denial of how bad he was. I told myself he can't be that bad. He goes to work everyday. He comes home and is always there for me. Since I had gone through so much with my family, I was afraid I would lose him. I felt that he was using me as a crutch. I was drained mentally. He cried all the time. Sometimes he would sit on the bed and point towards the closet. He would tell me there were people in the closet. I would become frightened. I did not know what to do. Other times, when he was driving on the road, he would always have to stop to urinate. His bladder was getting bad from the alcohol. At night, instead of going to the bathroom, he would urinate in the draw. I knew that eventually I was leaving him, but did not know how. I was no longer happy with him. I was at a loss.

Bob taught me so many things in life. He showed me how to get over my fear of flying on a plane. He showed me how to face the tragedies that my family had been through. How to be a good printer. He was my everything. Now everything was tumbling down. I felt I had to get away, because of his drinking. I had no one except for my daughter Kim, and she was only a small child. Even though she was a child, I did get encouragement from her. I knew I had to do better for her and myself, no matter how much I loved Bob.

Bob was terminated from the Tennessee branch. I spoke to my friend Aida, in New Jersey. She and her husband had a thirteen room house. She asked us to move in with her. Bob rented a U-hall truck to move all of our furniture. I followed him in my Mustang from Tennessee to New Jersey, with my three year old daughter Kim. We arrived approximately three days later. On our way there Bob brought a bottle of whiskey. I talked him into giving it to me. I took one drink and threw it out. I realized when I took that drink that I was getting pretty bad myself. I never drove and drank, and I did it that day. If I had not thrown the bottle away, we never would have arrived safely.

We stayed with Aida and Louie for about four months. We were in Toms River New Jersey and jobs were hard to come by. I mailed six resumes to different companies for Bob. I inquired for office work but nothing was available. A printing company from Jersey City answered one of Bob's resumes. We moved from Aida's house and rented an apartment in Bayonne, New Jersey, which was close to the printing company in Jersey City. Bob started working as a Printer. It was a good company and the money was fairly good. He worked for about six months, and started drinking on the job again. Kim was four years old and had her friends come over to play. On more than one occasion Bob was passed out on the floor when her playmates came over to play. The children had to walk over him to get to the back yard. One particular day I was very upset about this. The next day I told him he had to go for some type of help. I took him to Lyons hospital, New Jersey. I had him admitted. I was driving with one hand, while I had the other hand holding him down in the back seat. He wanted to stop for a drink. I convinced him that I could not stop. At the hospital he gave me a hard time until the doctor talked him into staying. When I returned home, I received a call saying that he had walked out of the hospital after three hours.

He came home and was smoking and drinking all day. He laid on the sofa in a stupor. I thought to myself, I wanted out, and I wanted out bad. I took Kim and drove to my brother Johnny's house. I was not going back. I left all my furniture and my possessions. I could just see him burning up the apartment. I called his sister. She told me to take out my furniture because he would probably sell it.

The next day I went to Paterson, New Jersey to look for an apartment. I rented an apartment, also rented a truck and between Johnny, a friend, and myself moved the furniture out of the apartment. I left him a bed, T.V. and a dresser. The day I walked out on Bob was one of the hardest decisions I had ever made in my life. I took Kim to Johnny's house. After I dropped her off, I went to the cemetery where my mother was buried. I drove for half hour and could not find the burial plot. I was crying and extremely upset. I bent down on my knees and prayed for my mother to help me. I was a nervous wreck. I calmed down after I was there for a while. I then drove to my stepfather's house in the Bronx. He was glad to see me, as we were very close. I took a hot bath. My body was still shaking from the big decision I had made. I felt better being with my stepfather Camilo. I stayed with him for a couple of days. I returned to New Jersey to get Kim.

Kim and I moved to Paterson, New Jersey. I did not know one soul in the area. Still I was determined to go on with my life. I learned that I could get on with life on my own. I had Jesus and faith to guide me. Also, that I had Kim to live for. Having Kim meant the world to me. It was easier than I had anticipated.

I applied for a secretarial position in Shulton Products, Clifton, New Jersey. Shulton Products manufactures Old Spice products. That was the start of a challenging career for me. I worked in International Market Research and was employed by Don Judd, Helen Berry and Jay Danish.

I enrolled Kim in a Day Care Center, close to my job. I was proud that I had accomplished so much in such a short time. I had been with Bob for sixteen years. At this point all I ever really missed was someone hanging up the pictures. So I learned how to put up my own nails and pictures. I had prepared myself in the earlier years of my marriage to become independent.

I received a call from Johnny at 2:00 a.m. in the morning. He told me that my father had been hit by a car. He was in critical condition. I was so upset that I went to my altar at home and broke St. Joseph's statue of course I later regretted it, but the damage was already done. I prayed for hours. At 5:00 a.m., he called back and said my father had passed away. It was a hit and run. He had been struck in the Pancreas. He was seventy seven years old. He had been visiting his lady friend at the funeral parlor. When he left to go home he crossed the street and was hit by the car. He was thrown up into the air about four feet. He never had a chance. The only one left of our family was my brother Johnny.

I started dating and met a fellow named Jay. The first thing he mentioned was marriage. He had recently gotten divorced. He had a nine year old son. I filed for divorce in 1974, so I could be free to marry Jay. We dated for a year and a half. After I got my divorce, Jay never spoke about marriage again. He brought it up at the beginning of the second year. I laughed and said "I don't want to get married now"!

Kim was doing well in school. She had a high I.Q. and was a beautiful little girl. I always gave her beautiful birthday parties. I would dress her in red and white dresses for the parties. The colors looked perfect on her because of her blonde hair and blue eyes.

At the beginning of the third year of living by myself I wanted to settle down because I was feeling lonely. I met Willie at a night club in the Bronx. He worked for his uncle in a restaurant. He lived with him. He was from Puerto Rico and had only been in the United States for a year. After we dated for a short while, he said he wanted to marry me. I now realize that most men say this so that they have a better chance at a relationship. As if I needed another marriage. Kim did not like him from the beginning. She was five years old at the time. She sensed something about him that I didn't.

After three years, I moved from Paterson, New Jersey to the Bronx, New York. I moved into an apartment with Willie. What a big mistake that was. A mistake that I would regret for the rest of my life.

I thought Kim did not like Willie because he did not speak much English. I thought she would get used to him.

Willie got a job at a factory. He did not have much going for him. He was what I call a hick from Puerto Rico. The type that expects the wife to do everything for him. He spoke no English and was very loud. He rented a grocery store and went into business. I told him I was unable to have children. He told me that he would get me pregnant. After four months of living with him, I became pregnant. The first four months we were happy. After that, I realized he drank everyday. I could see my happy days lessening. I would lay in bed and think, not again! My only blessing in this relationship was that I had become pregnant. He told my friend Aida that he did not want the baby. I would never have had an abortion, and I told him so.

Willie, did not wear pajamas to sleep. He covered

himself with a large sheet and walked throughout the house. One night, Aida came to spend the night. She noticed Willie coming out of Kim's bedroom. He had been in there for about one-half-hour. The next day I approached Willie about what Aida had told me. He told me he was praying beside Kim's bed, as his father often did when he was a little boy. I believed him, because I was naive and I trusted him.

I quit work because of my pregnancy. When Willie opened the store, he put the store under his name. Believe me, it was his store, not mine. I was not included in the business transactions. He used me to work in the store. His brother had the combination for the safe. I did not even have that. For someone who did not have much going for him, he surely surprised me. He was a sneaky person. He had me ask all my male friends to help him build the interior of the store. Since he did not speak English, I took care of the checks, the details of the business. When he started to make money, I was not included.

At the beginning of the relationship, he attemped to hit me a few times. He saw that I would not put up with it, so he stopped. He was abusive to me. I started to lose my self-esteem. I would go to the grocery store for food. He would insult me in front of the customers. I would walk out with my head down.

I had always been such a proud person, I walked with my head held high, and now I was always walking with my head down.

One night we were held up in the grocery store. We were all at the store. My daughters, myself, Willie and his cousin. When the men came in, one of them held a gun and pointed it straight at Kim. She gave him all the money because she happened to be at the cash register. She was only nine years old.

The other man held his gun straight at me. Serena, the baby was crying. The dog was running back and forth. Willie and his cousin went into the back of the store, to call the police. They did not come out until the thieves had left. When I told him that he was a coward, he tore the sleeve off my blouse. He was forever giving the police freebees, therefore, they were always on his side, whenever we had domestic problems. I approached Kim one night as we were sitting on the stoop. I asked her if anyone had ever touched her intimately. She said no. Then I asked her if Willie had ever touched her. She said no. She was nine years old at that time. I explained to her about grown-ups touching children intimately and if it ever happened to her, she should let me know. A young girl's mother came into the store and said Willie had promised to give her daughter groceries for free. The girl was about fourteen years old. The mother was not upset, but I sure was. Another occasion, my niece Diana, came to stay with us for a few days. She was seventeen years old. She left sooner than I expected because Willie was playing music and asked her to dance while I was out working. She told me she didn't like him.

I went to the dentist. When I got home, I went to bed because of the Novocaine. When I awoke, I went to the living room. Both Kim and Willie were watching T.V. Kim was laying on the sofa and Willie was stroking her leg. I asked him what was he doing? He said "nothing". After that incident I did not sleep very well. I would get up every two hours to make sure everything was allright. I could not believe that this man, whom I thought I loved, could be a child molester. I started to read documents on child molestation. I wanted to talk to someone about my suspicions, but did not know whom to speak to. I never did catch him doing anything, but he was showing signs of a very sick individual. He was drunk most of the time and working in the store, therefore I could not see his behavior when he was away from me. When he left to go to work, I would approach him about different incidents that were bothering me about himself. He would be sober at the time and he would say that it was all in my mind. That he wouldn't think about bothering little girls.

    The day I had Serena was a happy and very sad day. When I went to the bathroom I was spotting red. I knew this was not normal. It was two weeks before my due date. I called Willie to come home and take me to the hospital. When he arrived at the apartment, he said, "I am going to take a shower and put on a suit." I told him the doctor wanted me there right away. He took his shower and put on his suit and two hours later we left for the hospital. When we arrived I was in a great deal of pain. The doctor told me that I needed a caesarean section because I had placenta previa, which means that the placenta was coming out before the baby. The doctor put me under anesthesia. I was very frightened because the nurse put the clamp on my thigh, instead of the curtain beside my bed. Everyone was in a state of confusion. I therefore felt like this was the end.

    When I came to, Willie was by my side. He told me that Serena weighed only one and a half pounds. I could not believe this was possible. Luckily, the previous day, I read an article in the paper about a baby born at two pounds and she had survived. I did not see Serena for a few days. I thought she had died and they were keeping it from me. I prayed as I never had before. In my mind, I saw little angels flying around my bed, therefore, within my heart, I felt she was alive. I was unable to get out of bed to go see her because of the caesarean. When I saw her for the first time, I thought I was going to faint. She was so tiny and hooked up to so many different machines. She had jaundice and her eyes were covered so the light would not bother her. She was in an incubator. After the initial shock of her being so tiny, I was able to accept it. I gave her formula from an eyedropper. The first time I picked her up her pamper slipped off. It was too big for her. I went home and had to leave her for forty days. I went to see her every day. The doctor told me that she might have water in her head. I took her home and I was a nervous wreck. She cried more than most babies cry. I took her for a test to see if she had water in her head. The test was negative. Serena started to gain weight and was doing well. She did need lots of tender love and care. She was a slow learner, but after the age of two, she started to catch up to most babies. She had blue eyes and blonde hair. Just as my older adopted daughter, Kim. Willie always said he wanted two daughters with blonde hair and blue eyes. Now he had them. They did not look like me because I have brown hair. On my mother's side there is fair complexion and blue eyes, and on his side, his grandmother is fair with blonde hair. When I took my daughters out people often remarked about how cute they were. They always asked about why they were so fair. I would say, jokingly, "their father is the milk man." They would look at me strange and walk away.

Our family life was not good. Willie was working at the store from seven in the morning until one at night. I would put Serena on the school bus in the morning and walk Kim to school. I cooked, cleaned, and took care of the children. He was demanding on how things should be done at home. He was always telling me what to do to take care of the kids and cook the food, even though he was always at the store. He would come home drunk, at one in the morning, and tell me to wake the girls so they could eat dinner at that time.

I did not realize that Willie was such a strange person. I sometimes wonder if he was abused as a child. He never did tell me. When Kim was twelve years old, she told me that Willie had been molesting her since she was six. I was cooking at the time. She was crying. I calmly told her I would not do anything to him. I guess she got scared when she saw the look on my face. I told her I was going to the store for food. It was about seven in the evening. When I walked in and went behind the counter. My daughter Serena was with me. Him and his brother were behind the counter. He started yelling at me, why was I there so late at night and not home cooking. He didn't like me to go to the store. He did not want me to see him drink and know what he was up to. I said I wanted to get chicken to cook. I looked at the big knife and thought about putting it through his heart, then I picked up the smaller knife and stuck it in his arm. I told him this is for hurting my daughter. I grabbed Serena's hand and walked out. Serena thought the blood was tomato sauce. I felt bad for her having to witness this. She was three years old. I felt awful. I felt that I was a bad person. I went home and fell on my knees in front of the altar. I begged God to take me out of this hell and to please forgive me for what I had done. I thanked him for not letting me stab him in the heart, otherwise I would go to jail for murder. Who would take care of my children? I finally put my daughters to bed and fell asleep next to them. He never came home that night. The next day I took a shopping cart and went to the store to get the food that was rightfully mine. He was shocked to see me. I told him I was there for food. When he lifted his arm, he was in pain. He still denied doing anything to Kim. I practically emptied out the store and went home. From that day on things were different. He was afraid and I was determined to get out and start a new life.

When I reported it to the police they did nothing. They all thought he was a nice guy. He had most people fooled.

I did not want to continue in this relationship, but could not see any way out of it. Willie was very threatening, domineering, and impossible to live with. We had no family life. The only day we really celebrated was Christmas, and he still would not leave the store to come home, which was fine with me.

I worked at the store part-time. I applied for a part-time secretarial position at the church. I worked for a group of nuns. This is what kept my sanity intact. I cooked, cleaned, and took care of my daughters. I hired a part-time babysitter while I worked.

I started drinking heavily and felt awful about my life. I was not allowed to drink in the evening, even though he came home fighting every night. He complained about the cooking, the house being dirty or whatever he felt like. Nothing pleased him. He would start drinking early in the morning until about midnight. I started going to the bar because I was so tired of being by myself. I left Kim, the oldest, taking care of Serena. They would play and watch T.V. I still had no business leaving them alone. I was planning in my mind how I could get away from him. I even met two friends who were willing to defend me, if I needed help, if he tried to hurt me.

Working for the two nuns got to be too much, so I quit. I started going to A.A. meetings. I went into twelve detoxes, three rehabilitation programs and a half-way house. I was really in bad shape. I could not stop drinking on my own.

Before I went to all these programs, Willie kidnapped Serena and sent her to Puerto Rico to live with his parents. I thought I was loosing my mind. I would wait for the school bus everyday at 3:00. No Serena. I still did not know he had sent her to P.R. Serena did stay in P.R. for three years. Now I cared even less about my life. I called her every day and we would talk for a long time.

I finished the detoxes, and programs but still could not stop drinking. I left Kim with my brother Johnny, when I was going through all this. After awhile, Johnny could no longer watch her because he said she wasn't listening. He then sent her to my cousin in Baltimore.

I finally called the police and they removed Willie from the house. I now had the apartment for Kim and myself. My friend, Cliff came around everyday to make sure I was all right. Willie showed up through the fire escape and Cliff was at the apartment. Cliff told him to stay away from me. He was such a coward, he did not show up again.

Eventually, I was evicted because my rent was behind, he didn't even pay that. I was on welfare. I went to my friend Frank's house to stay for a while. He was the best friend I ever had. After awhile, I went to my friend Lydia's house. Her and my sister had grown up together. They were best friends. Lydia told me that my friends were no longer around, but she would always be my friend. I stayed with her for a couple of months. She helped me get into a hospital for my drinking. She never did give up on me. She was there for me always and still is. I, in turn, have been there for her. Good friends are hard to come by. I knew her since the age of five.

I met Jorge when I was forty-five years old. I went to Brooklyn to find out about a half-way house for alcoholics. All the other programs I had attended failed, I decided to try this half-way house. This house was designed to teach an individual to stay sober. Upon graduation you should be prepared to face the world on the outside again. I recall walking from the train station to the address I had on a piece of paper. I had my suitcase and was very frightened of what lay ahead of me. All of a sudden, I see this man running toward me from the corner of the block. He asked me if I needed help. I was looking at a building to see if I had the right address of the house. When I found the address he said "Oh man, I live there." He seemed happy to know I was going to live there. I felt relieved to find out that I had met someone from the house. He was very cute and spoke Spanish. We walked into the building and I spoke to the receptionist. I later found out that Jorge was only twenty-seven. When he found out I was 45 years old he said there was no problem with the age difference. I did not agree. I felt very old and sick at the time. In the beginning, I ignored him. After awhile that was difficult to do. It was a co-ed environment. There were three floors. The kitchen and recreation areas were on the first floor. The second floor was for the women. The third floor was for the men. We had A.A. meetings every day. One in the morning and one at night. We had chores assigned to each of us. We had group therapy sessions every day. At night we watched television and relaxed. Wherever I was sitting Jorge would pop up next to me. It seemed that I could not avoid him. I was in a ten month program. The first three months, I kept to myself. I always went to my room after each session. I read a lot. I did not socialize with anyone. I was confused because both my daughters were now living with relatives. I missed them tremendously. I cried all the time. Kim was fourteen and Serena was six. I felt as though I would never see them again. Eventually, Jorge and I became good friends. We would discuss our drinking days and how much pain we felt within ourselves. I was not interested in him as a man, but as a friend. I was at the house for my sobriety and only my sobriety. At nights, we would go for walks and argue most of the time. Basically, we were both unhappy about how our lives had turned out. We also encouraged each other about the future. I made a few friends, but did not trust anyone but Jorge. He would sometimes bring a gift to my door. He was doing this so that I would come out and socialize with everyone. Eventually it worked.

I went to see my counselor after my three month period. I had packed my bags and was ready to leave. I told him I wanted to go home. I told him I did not want to stay for the ten month program. He asked me if I wanted to go back to the hell I was in with Willie. If I wanted to drink for the rest of my life? If I wanted my children back? Did I want to be happy again? I realized that the questions made sense. Right then and there I decided, no matter what, I wanted to live sober again and be with my two beautiful daughters. Willie wanted to reconcile with me. I told him "no way." After all that he had put me through, it was out of the question.

After speaking to my counselor, I decided to give the program my all. I started staying out of my room and socializing with the other people. I listened more at the meetings. I participated in all the activities. I even joined the Catholic Church across the street and became a Lector. The church had been what attracted me to the house in the first place.

One night Jorge and I went to a movie. He kissed me good-night and I said "wow"! I still did not want to get serious, but it happened anyway. He graduated before I did. He got a furnished room a few blocks away. He visited me often. When I graduated, I got a room in the YMCA. Jorge asked me to move in with him. He told me eventually we would get my daughters back. I gave it some thought. I finally said yes. I told Willie it was over and started my life with Jorge. I prayed that it would work out. I was so tired of the suffering, pain and abuse that I had with Willie. Jorge and I left Brooklyn and got a furnished room in the Bronx.

Jorge was a hardworking man and he took good care of me. He saved money to bring Serena back from Puerto

Rico. We soon found an apartment and bought furniture. The apartment was in the Bronx.

We brought Serena home and then Kim came from Baltimore. I was ecstatic to have my family back again. I even got my dog Wendy back. I prayed with all my heart for this moment and I knew that God had heard me and for that I was so grateful.

We lived in the apartment for one year and found it was infested with drug addicts among other things. Most of the people were doing crack cocaine. I called my brother, Johnny, in New Jersey. He told me that he had an apartment with two bedrooms. We moved that same week. We did not own a car so we moved all our worldly possessions on the train. I registered Serena in Catholic school. Kim had already finished school in Maryland. Serena adjusted better than Kim did. Kim was very rebellious. After what happened with Willie, I couldn't blame her. She was staying out late. Serena started to date a boy who was nineteen years old. I told him to stay away from her, but he still hung around outside of our house. I finally took him to court. He stopped coming around. Serena's grandmother came to the States for a visit. She convinced Serena to move back to Puerto Rico and finish school. Serena did not like the schools in New Jersey so she left and has been there ever since. She started college and got married. She now has 2 children. She is very happy.

Kim was dating a boy named Eddie. She had a baby boy from him. Kim is now living with a man named Keith. She is also very happy. She deserves her happiness after all the misery that she went through with Willie.

It was not easy at the beginning of our relationship because Jorge had never been married or had children of his own. He tried to discipline the girls, but that did not go well. We all cared about each other, but we did not have that certain closeness that goes with a family. He tried, the girls tried, and God knows I tried. He was not mature enough to take over a family. When Kim had her baby, Erik, we were overjoyed for the new addition. Even though she was single, we decided to make the best of it.

I had been with Jorge for about six years when I received a call that my ex-husband Bob had passed away. He met an Indian woman with two grown sons. She had AIDS. He contracted AIDS from her and passed away shortly after. I did not keep in touch with him after the divorce. Needless to say, I was shocked. So was Kim. He left Kim $25,000. He left the same amount for his daughter from his previous marriage. No matter what happened between us, he was a good person who didn't deserve to die the way he did. It was a shame he suffered so much.

I had been sober for about six years and was doing well with my sobriety. On the other hand, Jorge was not doing so well. He would go on binges about every six months. Luckily for me, he only drank for three or four days at a time. His body could not take the abuse of the liquor for longer than that. Then he would be all right for about eight months. In the meantime, it would destroy me because I would think of my awful past with my two ex-husbands. The difference was they did it every single day. The memories were so bad for me and I also thought I would pick up a drink. Thank God I never did. I have been sober now for twenty two years. I have also been with Jorge for the same amount of time. I do not know if Jorge has kept me sober or the greater higher power, I believe it is a little of both. It was not easy for me at the beginning but I knew I had given up too much. I had also been very close to death because of the drinking. I was not going to be a victim anymore.

When we arrived in New Jersey, neither one of us had

a driver's license. Jorge was the first one to get his. It was difficult for him because his reading was not good and he needed to pass a written test. Kim helped him practice on a tape recorder. The test was difficult, but he finally passed it. His reading did improve because of that test. He did not have a trade. He attended welding school and graduated. He had different jobs in the beginning. He was not skilled enough for anything in particular. He then went into the maintenance field. He did very well in that field. He worked himself up to Director of Maintenance in a Nursing Home. He was not a quitter and has always worked and provided for the family. I have also helped him out financially. I finally got my license back and Jorge bought me a car. I did go back to work as a secretary and printer, but I didn't work steady because of the arthritis so I went on disability.

Through the years we grew and matured to a great extent. Especially Jorge. He has learned to accept the problems of everyday living. He is more understanding and considerate. We never had a child and I feel bad for him. I guess it wasn't meant to be. God does things for a reason. With all the other situations, we were just not ready for a baby.

We enjoy going to the movies, bowling, amusement parks, and living a clean and sober life.

I went to computer school in 1998. At first I hated computers because I did not understand them. The course took seven months. The first month, I did not do well. After that I did improve and was determined to learn the course. The teachers were very good. I went to Solution Learning in Edison, New Jersey. I was so proud of myself when I graduated and so was my family.

At that time I was diagnosed with Bipolar Disorder. It is not an easy illness to live with. It has to do with the brain not functioning properly. This happens periodically. I could not eat, laugh, cry, sleep, when I was depressed. If I was not depressed, I was manic. Manic is a feeling of being high. I would go from one extreme to another. I had to be hospitalized about ten times. I was given so many kinds of medications and some would help and others didn't. My daughter Kim took me to a hospital in her area and was finally given the right medication. This was a very difficult time for me and my family. The doctor told me that I would have this illness for the rest of my life. Well he was wrong because when the new doctor gave me the right medication, I can honestly say that I am feeling like a new person. Not only has the medication helped, but I know that Jesus healed me and heard my prayers seeking his help with this horrible illness. I always had faith in the Lord. Now I have a greater faith in God and Jesus because I know they are the ones that truly did heal me. Jorge was by my side and always there for me throughout this nightmare. I would console myself by looking at other people that were going through life with so many terrible illnesses and would tell myself "Gloria consider yourself lucky that it could have been worse". I feel this was caused by all the drinking I did throughout my life.

We did buy a house. It is a two family house. We just love it. If my daughters ever want to come home, they are always welcome. Jorge and them have a better understanding of each other now. Even though we never had children, he does consider my daughters and grandchildren part of his life.

In 1991 my ex, Willie went to live in Puerto Rico with his parents. He got cirrhosis of the liver. He was hospitalized. I received a call from Serena that he had tubes inserted in his stomach. He pulled them out and choked to death.

Jorge does not drink at all which is a blessing. I finally found the happiness I longed for with Jorge. I put all the years that I suffered behind me. With the help of God and Jesus, I survived. I am now sixty five years old and at peace with my life. My daughters are doing good and so are my grandchildren.

Not long ago I had a terrible cough and could not breathe at all. I called the ambulance and they took me to the hospital. I did not want to tell my family since I was always sick with one thing or another. They diagnosed me with Asthma, Bronchitis, and Pneumonia. They were not helping me at all. I still could not breathe. I went home sick and decided to go to a better hospital. This was a better hospital but they still were not sure of what I had. My doctor came to see me and told me he was going on vacation. He left his assistant and he could not tell me what was wrong with me. Needless to say I was very upset and took a taxi to go home. When I arrived home and told Jorge what happened, he started yelling at me and told me to go back to the hospital. I yelled back and then he pushed me. I called the police. When they arrived the lady police officer called me into my room. The two officers were in the living room with Jorge. I heard him tell them that I had Bipolar Disorder. I started to come out of the room and the officer pushed me back into the room. She did not want me to go into the living room. I told her "this is my house and I can go anywhere I want to". Then the two officers came over and put the handcuffs on me and told me that I was under arrest. I asked them to please put the handcuffs in the front because I was sick and it was very painful for them to put them in the back. I feel very bad when my family speaks about the Bipolar Disorder. Jorge told them not to hurt me. They took me down to the car. The officer said that he was going to throw me face down into the car. They took me to the police station and never read me my rights. They did not let me use the telephone to call anyone.

Here I was sixty five and in jail. They left me in a room and completely ignored me. Every time an officer went by I would ask him how much was my bail and they would just keep walking. After about three hours they let me make a telephone call. I called my daughter. I did not sleep and the next day they gave me breakfast. I did not eat it. They then took me to the prison in Elizabeth. I was there for one day. Jorge and my daughter came that night and bailed me out. They kept my glasses so I could not see the names of the officers. They also kept forty five dollars of mine. The bail was six hundred and fifty dollars. I was given a court date. I went to court about five times. They accused me of assaulting the police officers. I was unable to pay for an attorney so I asked for a public defender. She was very good and they dropped the charges. I went to a different doctor and he told me that I had emphysema. I had been smoking for about forty years. He gave me a few different kinds of medications and I can finally sleep nights without coughing and can now breathe better again. I have not smoked for a year. It was not easy to stop, but after the third week I learned how to live without it. I do not miss it at all.

I am now doing volunteer work in a church as a secretary. I just love it. I feel even closer to the Lord and I am more positive of everything that is now happening in my life. Jorge brought me a Amazon parrot and she is beautiful. She makes me feel so good and keeps me a lot of company. I feel as though I am starting to live my life all over again because I feel very content and happier. I am also looking younger because I really work at it. I have always been young at heart, therefore, I should try to look younger. By the way, my Parrot's name is Rainbow. She says "I love Rainbow"! When I wake up in the morning, I always say, " This is the day the Lord had made; we will rejoice and be glad in it." I also told my daughters to do this and live one day at a time with the Lord.

Printed in the United States
60773LVS00004B/17